THE WAITRESSING BIBLE:
The only pocket guide you'll ever need to being the best
waiter you can be while maximizing your tips

DAVON THOMAS

ISBN:1461153913
ISBN-13: 9781461153917

DEDICATION

I dedicate this book to this book to my sister, who never stops having fun on the job. I also dedicate this book to everyone in the restaurant business. I'm honored to be serving you this time around.

CONTENTS

ACKNOWLEDGMENTS

I'd like to thank God, as well as my parents. Without either one of you this book wouldn't be. Much love, and many praises.

INTRODUCTION

First thing's first; congratulations! You have just brought the only guide you'll ever need to becoming the best waiter you can be! If you purchased this guide you most likely fall into one of three categories: either you are a waiter, aspiring to become one, or you would like to become more informed about the profession. Whatever the case may be. You'll be sure to find something helpful. Now, let me welcome you to the cash cow position of the restaurant industry. But only the waiter with a complete knowledge of the serving craft will be able to milk this cow dry, tip after tip, night after night, day after day. Besides, if you're going to do anything, you may as well do it right. Waitressing is an incredibly fun job especially if you have the right attitude! It can be nerve wracking on the weekends for sure, but the most important part is to have FUN! And as for the making money part, I'll teach you about that! Making good tips comes with making the right choices each step of the way. You must be ready by now. So here we go.

THE TWO LITTLE HUGE THINGS YOU NEED TO KNOW BEFORE YOU READ ON

There are some points that waiters should be privy to before pressing on:

There is a lot of variation on what a "waiter" should be referred to. Some believe that a "server" should be referred to in gender specific terms. For males "waiter" For females "waitress". This is dependent upon the social, and political climate of your environment. On a bigger note, it's also a matter of personal preference in which word you choose to describe yourself. In this book I will refer to any "server" as a "waiter", without regards to gender. It's entirely up to you to decide what you'd like to be called.

There has been a change in the restaurant industry in reference to what a person, or a person, who chooses to eat at your restaurant, should be called. Using the word "customer" to refer to this person, or persons is not only outdated, but also devalues their real worth to your restaurant's establishment. So with this in mind it's your duty to call anyone who decides to dine at your restaurant your "Guest", and they should be treated as such.

"People will call you many things, but it's what you call yourself that matters."

MISSION STATEMENTS

Every corporation has a mission statement. A mission statement is a written purpose, created as an invisible guiding force behind each decision made by that company, or entity. Corporations in the food industry are no different. Check out some of the mission statements I've chosen. These are some true words of wisdom from some of the biggest players in the game.

"To ensure that each guest receives prompt, professional, friendly and courteous service. To maintain a clean, comfortable and well-maintained premises for our guests and staff. To ensure that all guests and staff are treated with the respect and the dignity they deserve...
-- Brannigan's Restaurant

"To provide an exceptional dining experience that satisfies our guests grown-up tastes by being "Cut-Above" in everything we do."
--Arby's

"A Passion to Serve."
--Ninety-Nine Restaurant

"Every guest who chooses Culvers leaves happy."
--Culvers

"We pledge to make Yoshinoya the best place to eat and the best place to work."
--Yoshinoya

"Something for Everyone..."
--Cheesecake Factory

"Our aim is to provide happiness and joy through food..."
--Heart and Soul

"We are always focused on satisfying the needs of our customers and guests."
--IHOP

"To always remain at the peak in providing customer satisfaction, excellence at all cost, while we build a strong character and leaves an indelible impression in the heart of our client or associate."
--Sizzlers

"Passion is people."
--Ruby Tuesday

As soon as you decide to become a waiter, your restaurant's mission becomes your mission. It simply wouldn't be a business that anyone including you would want to eat at without these principles. This is what keeps guests coming back, and money coming in. Let these statements guide all of your decisions.

TURNING YOUR SWAGG ON A.K.A. ATTITUDE

Your swagg is your attitude. And your attitude is important because it's what makes, and breaks your whole career experience. It's the sole ingredient that can turn what you consider "work" into simply having fun on the job. You want to have fun on the job, and get paid to do it. Attitude includes body language, and state of grace toward your guests, and everything else in the restaurant. How you carry yourself. Your image. This is what will set you apart from other waiters. Your confident, and you look confident. You have the attitude of a winner. Remember only you can truly let yourself go, and allow your personality to show. All I'm doing is showing you the way.

How would you like to be caught looking? Hopefully you've answered "as good as possible". When you're on the restaurant floor don't slouch, bend, or lean on anything. This looks unprofessional. There's always someone watching, especially your guests. Sorry if your paranoid, but this is a reality.

No huffing and puffing, or crossing your arms as a reaction to anything a guest asks you, your not in preschool anymore. Lets get it together.

If you're to cool to smile, then you don't belong in this business. Maybe try applying for the N.S.A, or the C.I.A or some other uptight government agency. If you want to work in this business prepare your facial muscles to stay in a smile. Even when you don't want to, or it's hard to, smile no matter what.

Sound and act like you care. Be attentive. This means enthusiasm. When you talk maintain eye contact. Occasionally drop cues of understanding when talking to a guest.

Your going to have guests, and I say guests, because your going to have some not so good experiences with guests on more than one occasion. This will happen, it's okay. What's not okay is that negatively affecting your attitude toward guests in the future.

Have pride in yourself. This will make you sincere in everything your doing from taking a guests order, to executing the smallest task.

Despite what you may believe about yourself, your personality is good for the job. Never change who you are as a person, but make adaptations in the areas that may need it. So that you can be better at communicating with people. After all people are your business.

Be humorous as much as possible. Learn to see a little bit of comedy in everything. Even when everything is going wrong.

Leave your problems at the door...where they belong. Negative energy is real, and can be carried in along with the your problems, along with everyone else's. How do you stop this? By simply not talking about your problems on the job. But you're certainly welcome to pick your problems right back up at the door, on the way out of work.

Believe it or not waiters communicate their attitude to their tables by cues that are not always verbal, body language means a lot. So If your having a good time your guests will pick up on that, and if you aren't, that that will be communicated as well. So make sure to have a good time.

You'll have good days, and bad ones, the better you get at being a waiter, the more good days, and less bad days there will be.

Have fun. Show your personality. Turn your swag on. It's that simple.

"It's a myth that we all must work for a living in this lifetime...Change your attitude, and you may find yourself having fun, and getting paid to do it."

HOW TO WIN THE INTERVIEW

So you got yourself an interview! Hooray! Good job! That was the hard part. Now, for the easy part...which will be easy since you'll be playing close attention to guidelines that will prove to be extremely helpful to you, come interview time. The interviewer is the gatekeeper; so let the interviewer know what a unique asset you are to their restaurant.

Don't come dressed laid back for an interview. Always come in wearing your best in business professional attire. You don't want to look like you could care less about the position your going for. So with that said no jeans, flip flops, clogs, and tank tops.

References should be varied. As well as good. Diversify them. Filling your references out full of friends might no be the wisest choice. A friend, a former manager, one from an educational institution, or trade organization. The choice is yours. Make sure their good ones. You don't want a reference that has the worst opinion in the world of you, because that wouldn't be beneficial to you.

"Your hired!" when the interviewer utters those two golden words, be happy, be very happy. But also be ready to sacrifice whatever leisure time, or weekends you may have to for the sake of the job, at least in the beginning. You don't want your employer not be able to use you as soon as possible.

Make sure you smile! Who can't appreciate a nice smile?

Make eye contact.

Be prepared for answering personal questions that probe your personality traits, qualities, likes and dislikes. "Have you ever stolen anything?" "Where have you worked previously?" "Do you have a criminal record?" "What's your experience in the food industry?" "Where do you see yourself in the future?" "Are you willing to work for the business a long time or is this a temporary job for you?" "Do you have reliable transportation?" "How are you with attendance?" And most likely scenario based questions; such as "what would you do in a given situation?" "How do you handle stress" "How would you react to an upset customer?" "Are you a team player?" "Are you flexible with your schedule?" Stay calm and be honest.

Think about why you'd like to work at that particular restaurant the night before the interview. Magnify your most positive qualities. If your outside the united states then bring the equivalent in information documents.

Don't forget to bring two forms of identification with you; your driver's license, and your social security card usually do the trick.

On the day of the interview look at what kind of restaurant it is your applying for, is it a five star restaurant? Whatever the case is, information like this will help you to know if the environment is right for you. For example, an uptight five star restaurant may not be the right place for you.

On the interview feel free to ask the interviewer questions; this isn't bending the rules in anyway. An interview gives you the chance to inquire about the establishment. There goals in the future, if they have other locations, the kinds of people that frequent their restaurant. And any other questions that you think would better help you choose the right restaurant for you. The interview isn't an interrogation! So don't view it as such! Being receptive, as well as asking questions, about the nature of what you're getting yourself into. This is a great quality in an employee. These qualities will get you far.

Go with your gut. If you feel that perhaps there's too much stress involved in your waitressing duties, then being a waiter may not be for you, and that's fine. There are tons of other fields in which to work! You're either right for the job, or your not. The choice is yours.

If you have a shady or shall I say ugly past work experiences, its better to explain what you felt went wrong with the situation to your employer...of course only IF it COMES UP IN THE INTERVIEW! Never volunteer information.

No over thinking your answers. Don't over think period! It tends to hurt your brain. It will cause you to stumble over words, and give off bad signs of nervousness.

An interview is a conversation.

Your not perfect so don't pretend to be, no one is. Don't give answers because you think it sounds good.

We live in the information age, so being truthful is important, because all of your answers can be verified, and checked.

In the event that you don't get hired, don't become depressed; instead pinpoint things that you could've done better in the interview, and schedule an interview with another restaurant. Keep trying. Don't give up!

"Either it's meant to be, or it isn't. If it isn't, move on to what is meant to be."

IMAGE IS EVERYTHING

The quote "don't judge a book by its cover" is a good, and noble outlook on the appearance of things, and individuals. Unfortunately, it's a virtue that not many guests may have when walking into your restaurant. Guests judge you based on how you look. When going to eat at your restaurant they will assume many things by the appearance of the things in their environment. That means not only you, but also their dining environment. However shallow you may think it, this is the name of the game. So lets play it well, dress for success. And keep up good appearances.

Appearance plays a big role in increasing your tips.

You don't have to paint your face with makeup. For all the women out there putting too much make up on might give off the wrong impression. Make up is acceptable but keep it light.

Hair is neat or presentable.

Smell good, a light perfume or cologne.

Hygiene is big in anyplace where food is present. This means no dirty hair, fingernails, clothes, and hands! Shower as often as possible.

Please refrain from touching your body while dealing with food. If a guest sees you touching your mouth, nose, pelvis. They're liable to make a disgusted face, and leave. And who could blame them?

If a sudden itch or bodily irritation occurs, simply tell a fellow coworker that you're going to the bathroom, take care of any problems. Then wash your hands!

Jewelry may or may not be acceptable ask a supervisor. If it is acceptable be modest.

Clean work apparel. Iron your clothes; you don't want to be known as the waiter with a thousand wrinkles.

Please, if you smoke find some way to get rid of the horrible cigarette smell that lingers on your clothes afterwards. Or just kick the habit altogether, mints wouldn't hurt either.

Don't wear a thong or low-slung jeans with your butt crack hanging out. Save provocative clothing for the nightlife, at the club. You don't want to make guests feel uncomfortable or threatened by your sex appeal.

"Image is everything, and sometimes things aren't what they seem. So where does that leave you? Just get yourself a full length mirror, and be brutally honest with self."

PREPARED FOR ANYTHING

Batman has a utility belt; James Bond has all the gadgets you can think of. So what you don't have the exotic cars that Bond has, or you're not a cape crusader. There's enough action in this business to keep you on your toes, and if your not saving lives, your saving people from having a bad night, or dining experience all together. With that being said here's what you'll need in your arsenal.

A small note-pad or medium sized one; try to avoid the huge ones that make you look like your going to draw your guest's self portrait. Also if you can find one with pocket slips for any pieces of paper you might need to store that works to your benefit.

A calculator. You can buy a simple one. One that does simple arithmetic. This way you don't have to buy an overly expensive calculator. Try fitting that into your budget, or your pocket. It's hard to do!

Pens, you're going to need a lot of them. You don't want to be at a table unable to take an order because you don't have any. Pens with a good grip, because calices hurt after a long shift of writing orders with pens that don't have a good grip.

Aprons. There are all kind of aprons: Economy Kitchen, Cornerstone and Port Authority Bib, Former V-neck Server, Bar Apron, White 4-way Apron, Half Length 2 Pocket Apron, Bistro Apron, Full Length Apron...should I go on? It's a waitress apron extravaganza. When shopping for an apron in the event that your restaurant doesn't provide you with one, or you just feel the need to have your own, you want to purchase one that falls under the name "Server Apron". When it comes to style, and color just make sure it coordinates. Black is usually the best color due to dirt no being able to show up as easily. Other colors are fine, check with your manager beforehand, because colors like neon pink might be a little too flashy.

Money pouch. In the United States most restaurants are still using their cash registers. Outside of the "states" however I'm aware that waiters are responsible for keeping their guests bill money, as well as tip money on their person. Buy a well made, non-see through money pouch if your restaurant doesn't provide you with one. Or once again, if you'd just like to have your own.

"I'm too paranoid not to be prepared for any, and everything. You could learn a thing or two from me."

SPEAK YOUR GUESTS LANGUAGE

Phrases that your guests will always love to hear no matter what the situation, you cant go wrong with responding to your guests with one of these lines...

"Not a problem"
"Absolutely"
"Thank You"
"I'll be back in a second"
"I can accommodate you"
"I apologize, is there anything I can do?"

It doesn't hurt to take time to understand different cultures as well.

Widely Spoken Languages

The ten most popular spoken languages are Mandarin Chinese, English, Hindustan, Spanish, Russian, Arabic, Bengali, Portuguese, and Malay Indonesian, French.

This is how you say Hello, and Goodbye in each of them if you should feel the urge to greet, or bid farewell to your guests if you realize they speak one of these languages.

Mandarin Chinese: Hello: nín hao
 Goodbye: zài huì

English: Hello: Hello,
Goodbye: Goodbye

Hindustani: Hello: namaste
Goodbye: Alvida

Spanish: Hello: holà
Goodbye: Adios

Russian: Hello: дравствуйте!
Goodbye: Poka

Arabic: Hello: Marhaba

Goodbye: MA'a salama

Bengali: Hello: Kemon Aacho
Goodbye: Nomoskaar

Portuguese: olá
Goodbye: adeus

Malay Indonesian: Hello: Halo
Goodbye: Selamat malam

French: Hello: Bonjour!
Goodbye: Au revoir

There's going to be a lot of words, and phrases being used inside your restaurant. Some you may be familiar with, and some you may not be familiar with. Don't worry I got you covered.

86

In the restaurant business this means your fresh out of whatever what was referred to. "Hold off on the chicken sandwich, it's been 86'Ed". You use this term with other waiter staff, never with the guest because they wouldn't know what you were talking about.

A Bring Back

This means any order that the guest has rejected for any reason. Usually because of things such as: undercooked, overcooked, it's taste is not to their liking, too spicy, the food is too cold, etc.

Appetizer

We all love our appetizers. It's the course you will be serving before you serve the main dish. These dishes are always smaller than the main course.

Babysitter

The babysitter is another word for Manager. It's a humorous title that pokes fun at the Supervisor who is looking after you all day long.

Back-Of-The-House

This term can mean a variety of things, but usually it's referring to the kitchen, or stock rooms.

Bill

Well this little piece of paper is what the total cost of all the purchases is written on. You may here a guest say "check please!" when they are ready for you to bring them the bill.

Buggin Out

For when you just cant take your career as a waiter anymore, and you go crazy cursing, being mean, your officially "buggin out".

Break Room

This one explains itself; waiters use this room to take a well-needed break from whatever chaos is going on outside or inside them. Feel free to gossip with other waiters, or just plain relax. If you want to smoke your better of doing that outside.

Busser

The busser is an employee assigned the sole duty of cleaning, collecting, and placing silverware on the table. Making sure the tablecloth is on, plates are distributed. Trash is cleaned off the table. Very nice waiters sometimes share in these responsibilities.

Check
This is just another word for "Bill".

Entree
The main course being served.

Folding Napkins
When you use a folded napkin to create a new form, shape, or object out of it. This new shape can be whatever your creative mind can turn it into. Mostly used as table decorations.

Front Of The House
What's not in "The Back Of The House" is in the front. The Hostess is usually stationed here.

Guest
A guest is someone or persons who have decided to dine at your restaurant.

On The Fly
Usually your shouting this at the kitchen staff because you need the dish fast.

Hostess
This person seats your guests at open tables.

Regular
Any guest, or group of guests who frequently dines at your restaurant.

Server
Just another way of saying waiter, some guests will use this term.

Shift

The time you start working till the time you stop. This is on a day-to-day basis. A shift is composed of your hours, or "day time shift", "night shift", "lunch shift".

Tip
Now as a waiter this will be one of your favorite words, because this is the money a guest gives to you, at the end of their stay. In the United States its usually 15 to 20 percent. Although these percentages may vary from country to country.

Waitron
This can be used in reference to a waiter, or a waitress.

Waiter
Some refer to male servers as waiters.

Waitress
Some guests may refer to female servers as a waitress.

"If loving care is not the universal language. Then it most definitely should be."

DO'S AND DON'T'S

There are things that can make, or break you in this business, beware the pitfalls. The right "do" can get you the hefty tip you deserve. The wrong "don't" and you might not receive a tip at all. Pay attention.

Celebrities. Don't spaz when you see a celebrity, start asking him/her questions about their personal life; like who their going out with, why they did what they did to make money, etc. Keep your composure, and treat them like any other guest.

Special moments. Don't interrupt a guest with questions if they have a fork full of food in their mouths; or if they're in the middle of a conversation. Timing is everything, and you don't want to ruin a special moment.

Do walk past your guest's table just to let them know your checking up on things. If you see something that needs tending to: such as an empty plate, a glass that needs to be refilled, then do so. Most of the time if the guest sees you, and they need something they wont hesitate to ask.

Watching your mouth And Your Temper. Don't under any circumstances curse out, yell, or bad mouth guests.

Never Assume Anything. Don't ask a guest the "Do you need change with this?" There are so many things wrong with this statement. This tends to make a guest feel obligated to tip the amount of the change left over. A better method is to just skip this question, bring back the guests due change, and if the guest wants you to have it they will give it to you. Which is much better than you indirectly pressuring them.

Don't use words like "sweetie", "hunny", "sweetheart", "baby". These are either used primarily as pet names, or names for your "lover" which the guests are neither.

Treat every guest as you would your family, and if your friends or family decide to dine at your restaurant, no special treatment.

Do be able to give good honest meal recommendations.

Don't assume everyone will like a certain drink, entree, desert just because you enjoyed it. Everyone's tastes are different.

Do ask, "How was your day?" Because whether it was a good or bad day you're going to do your best to make their experience a great one.

Do anticipate needs. Have extra napkins, silverware, condiments close by. When a guest requests something bring more than enough.

Don't count your tips on the restaurant floor where guests can see you. Counting your money should always be done in private.

Don't hide from your table if the order is taking too long. The right thing to do is inform the guests as much as possible about the situation. You should even go as far as giving something "on the house" and apologizing for the delay.

Do invite your guests to come back if your service was good, then there's a good chance that they might request you by name.

After taking a guests order repeat the order back to them. This is a must. It prevents mistakes of a wide variety.

When it comes to serving alcohol, always i.d. your guests politely, don't just go on looks.

Do tell your guests if something isn't free or comes with a meal. That they will be paying for it.

Be prepared to customize a guests order.

"I don't control you, I don't even know you. But I do know your actions have been controlling your future ever since day one, and will continue to do so."

WAITER ETIQUETTE

Welcome to the waiters school of etiquette. General rules of thumb that every waiter should be aware of.

Always come back and ask, "How did the food turn out? Is there anything else I can get you?"

Know your menu back and front. Of course you don't have to study it as if you have to take a test on it, but look through it, paying attention to prices along with new meals. Also wines, and good drinking combinations.

Words like "Sir" and "Miss" are always better than pet names that might be inappropriate.

If your ever unsure of how a meal is served, always go, and make sure. Don't promise anything that you can't deliver.

When dealing with guests make eye contact with each of them. This allows each guest to feel acknowledged. You don't want any guest to feel left out, or invisible.

Never lean on a table while talking to a guest. Or anything that could make you look lazy. Stand upright while taking orders.

Take the time to do things right, but watch how much time you take on each task. Time is money. Never rush a guest no matter how rushed you feel.

Write neatly while taking orders. I know a few waiters who write so poorly they can barely read their own handwriting. This doesn't help anyone.

Simply apologize to a guest. Never under any circumstances give excuses for your mistakes.

Most guests appreciate a waiter who knows what they're doing. They usually show this appreciation come tip time.

As a waiter greet every guest that comes into your restaurant. No matter when, and where you encounter them.

"You're free to be as free spirited as you like, but you'll be fined a hell of a lot if you don't pay attention."

GUESTS COME IN ALL TYPES

One thing is certain in the serving profession you're going to meet all kinds of people, the world is filled with them. All different kinds, makes, and models. Know people, become wise, and profit from their wants, and needs.

Pay attention on a daily basis to who frequents your restaurant. These guests are known as "regulars" get to know them, and their favorite meals.

Take care of the kids, anytime you see children don't hesitate to bring anything that can entertain them. Coloring books, crayons, small toys if you have them.

Never judge a guest by what they're wearing. Don't treat anyone according to his or her looks, or how much money you think they have.

THE ANGRY GUEST

Its bound to happen once or twice. Either it is a guest who likes venting about their problems by being unsatisfied with your every move, or a guest who sees your service is in need of improvement, but lacks the communication skill set to do so effectively, or respectfully. Whatever the case may be. Here are ways to finesse the situation, and alleviate the tension.

When a guest is angry with you, and you want to react with even more anger, simply don't do it. What you want to do is become more gentle, and calm. Someone will have to calm down to alleviate the situation, make sure its you as much as possible.

If a guest appears to be a very needy person, give them exactly what they want, be extra attentive usually this treatment will cater to their ego.

Guests will usually react better to a bad situation if you offer something complimentary.

Never lose your patience or your cool.

"Two angry minds will never think of a peaceful resolution."

STRESS MANAGEMENT: YOUR GOING TO NEED IT

I'm not asking you to become a monk, but I am asking you to acquire some of the Zen, and patience they are famous for. Think it's too difficult? It's easier then you think! We all get angry or stressed out, it's human. The professional knows how transform, and evolve this basic instinct. To those waiters of practical solutions to the chaos that might be around them, they give order to their environment, with as less stress as possible.

Take deep breaths and find that inner peace whenever you feel overwhelmed.

When you have difficult guests don't take out your aggression on your coworkers.

Thinking ahead will always be helpful in stress reduction. It saves you from mistakes that you "might" have made. It keeps you from wasting energy that you "might" have saved.

Organization is powerful. Everything has a place.

"Any time your getting angry, just realize how calm everyone else is.

THE MENU

The bread, and butter of the restaurant. The menu is akin to your religion's most sacred book, now be a good practitioner, and learn the doctrine of your restaurants menu.

Know your menu frontwards and backwards. This includes drinks.

Understand your guest's intentions and needs. Mirror people. "Read" them understand their sense of humor and relate to them.

"Artists have paint pallets, you have a menu, with meals on it. Paint the perfect dining experience."

KEEP YOUR BALANCE: HOW TO MASTER CARRYING YOUR ORDERS

It's like you're in the circus. Juggling trays, drinks, requests, and orders. Your body isn't cooperating? How can I possibly carry all this; you find yourself thinking. Feeling like you need two extra sets of hands, and arms? I'll show you how to do fine using what you have.

Learn which arm is stronger, and use that arm more when handling trays, shift more of the weight to this arm.

Use your abdomen, as well as your chest. This is especially effective if you have weak wrists, or hands. Use your whole body, but stay away from using your shoulder. You don't want food close to your hair!

Using your fingers to grip a tray creates a stronger grip than using your palm underneath the tray.

The psychic energy you give anything while your concentrating strongly on it is called "focus". While walking with a tray in your hand whether its full of drinks, or food don't watch it. Why? You could focus on your tray so much you may not focus on what's in front of you!

If you have weak wrists the first thing you should do is practice carrying plates without any food on them at all.

Try to come up with, as many ways possible to balance plates while you're at home, this will build comfort, and creativity that will serve you well at the workplace.

When putting a dish on a table, first set down the edge of the dish this will avoid the dish shaking, as well as your arm. Then slide it gently fully onto the table.

"Stay away from extremes. Balance always brings happiness. Balance is also the difference between a guest's food on the floor, and on the table."

SO YOU'RE A VEGETARIAN

Great you're a vegetarian. The animals deserve someone in their corner, and so does mother earth, we do great damage to both animals, and our environment, blah, blah, blah. This is all great, and well. I'm sure you'll receive a thousand blessings, but venting your outrage in front of the guests because they enjoy meat in their meals is unprofessional. Be a political activist elsewhere. When you're at work, you're at work.

You don't have to try each meal yourself, and if you're a vegan you definitely won't be trying every meal, unless you're working at a vegetarian restaurant. So when giving recommendation to a guest, or guests, think about what meals are popular, and which meals have been receiving good reviews from other guests.

Dealing with a vast amount of meat eaters in the workplace might do a little harm to your beliefs, but you must use restraint, and distinction. Understand that everyone has different beliefs. Don't look at others with these different beliefs as attacking your own.

"Some things you keep to yourself, your better off that way."

EXERCISES

It's all about stamina, if you intend to stay in the game your entire shift, then your going to need a lot of it. Whether you have a routine exercise plan, or you just want to pump up the muscles that you find failing you on the job here are some workouts to consider:

You don't need to go out and buy a treadmill. But if you have one that's not a bad thing! Run on the treadmill for a fixed amount of time say, ten or fifteen minutes a day.

When doing your daily house cleaning or any kind of cleaning, do it quicker than usual; this will boost your heart rate. Makes for a convenient exercise.

If you have a staircase in the house, go up and down it a few times, I call it staircase aerobics.

If you don't have a staircase in your house, or apartment, jog around the block.

Go for a walk, you can walk at steady pace, or you can walk fast. Just make sure you push yourself a little bit out of your normal limits from time to time.

Ride your bike to work. Ride your bike to school. Ride your bike wherever, within your limits. I don't want you riding cross country, unless you want to, and the manager's willing to give you time off to do it.

Swimming a few laps around the pool, keeps your whole body toned as well as boosting stamina. If you're around the beach you can do it while catching a tan.

Wrists Exercises

You'll use your wrist everyday in your waiting career. Make sure they're getting the work out they need.

Wrist curls work great. Take two dumbbells; remember keeping your palms face up. Your arms should be at your sides, perpendicular to your body. Now using just your wrist raise the dumb bell to arm level. You can do this one at a time if you'd like.

Reverse wrist curls. The only difference between this exercise, and the wrist curl is that your palm will be facing downward instead of up.

When you brush your teeth, do it with both hands (meaning alternate hands). You get an ultra good cleaning, and a double wrist work out.

Make a fist out of both your hands (don't punch anyone's lights out) and rotate them from left to right. Due this for about five minutes a day.

Open palmed wrist circles. It's just like the circles you did with the fist, but with your hand stretched out, and loose.

Hand And Finger Exercises

Grippers are excellent for your hand strength, but I must warn you to stick to a moderate rate of workout, because it can turn your hands into crushing machines. If you're a female you might not want big bulky hands. You can buy them online, or offline at any sporting goods store.

"I think you look absolutely positively marvelous, but don't expect everyone else to think the same thing."

RELAXATION TECHNIQUES

Close your eyes. Breathe. Open your eyes. Conquer. Relaxation techniques can remedy nearly any unease you might be accumulating on a daily basis. Trust me if your going to be a waiter any length of time, you will be accumulating some unease. It can happen day or night.

If you have been effected by the following:

Nervousness, stress, rapid heart rate, high blood pressure, rapid breathing rate, minimal blood flow to muscles, muscle tension, chronic pain, low levels of concentration, anger, frustration, low levels of confidence, low self esteem...

Then the following techniques will benefit you greatly:

Technique #1

First find a quiet place. Find a comfortable place on your floor. Sit down close your eyes. Then repeat quietly, softly to your self "Tomorrow I will not become stressed when something goes wrong at work." Continue to chant this to yourself, while you do begin to imagine yourself in the middle of a peaceful forest. Focus your attention on your breathing; you want it to be relaxed. You can feel your heart rate slowing down. Allow your each limb to become relaxed, allow each part of your body to relax. Enjoy the physical sensations. You don't have to use the quote I supplied, feel free to customize, as you like until this technique suits you.

Technique #2

In this technique, you focus on slowly tensing and then relaxing each muscle group. This helps you focus on the difference between muscle tension and relaxation. You become more aware of physical sensations. One method is to start by tensing and relaxing the muscles in your toes and slowly work your way up to your neck and head. Tense your muscles for at least five seconds and then relax for thirty seconds, then do it all over again.

Technique #3

In this relaxation technique, you form mental images to take a visual journey to a peaceful, calming place or situation. This is a personal favorite of mine. The fun part about this is you can go anywhere; there is truly no limit to the places you can imagine. So lets choose the beach on a warm night for example. You can feel sand underneath your toes; the warm breeze sweeps over you. You can see how bright, and beautiful the moon looks hanging over the sea. All the sounds of the beach are calming; your eyes are closed as you become more, and more engrossed in your imagined experience. Interact inside your own world.

If the former techniques don't do the trick here are some activities that will be sure to get you relaxed:

Yoga, Tai Chi, listening music, exercise, meditation, hypnosis, getting a massage.

"Vacations are really inexpensive, all you have to do is sit down, shut up, and close your eyes."

WAITRESSING A TEAM SPORT

There's no "I" in team. You've probably heard that before. What I'm saying is you can't get very far alone. Everything depends on everything else, its the way of the universe, the way of the world, the way of life, so if you think your restaurant has escaped this universal law; your mistaken. You don't want to walk into a place ignorant of what makes it tick, do you? Think of this as the law of gravity, keeping you grounded. Waitressing may seem like an individual job, but actually, teamwork is a must if any waiter is going to make money and get along well with their coworkers.

Tip bartenders, bussers, and the hostess. When your coworkers workers see that they will be rewarded by you; This will definitely be an incentive for them to put helping you out as a high priority.

waitressing can be very frustrating, but don't take it out on hostesses and bussers. Treat the kitchen staff well. Don't yell at them!

Reward the staff for helping you get through a rough night in your own little way. Be creative.

Working as a team makes waiting tables way more fun, easier and financially rewarding. Everybody is making money. Laughing, and happy.

Help bus fellow waiters tables if your not doing anything.

If your feeling overwhelmed, and have too many tables at once. Let your coworkers know so that they can help you. Don't let pride keep you from working efficiently.

Your spending enough time at work you might as well make some friends.

"If you don't like the idea of a team because it involves more people than yourself, that sucks because you live in a world of billions."

ROOKIES

Rookies. Oh boy, (or girl) do I have advice for you. The restaurant business is tough and weekend based. Give up your weekends; give up your nightlife for a few weeks before requesting time off. Know your menu, know the seating, and know the drinks. Get to know a little bit about everything. Take some time and learn it! It all pays off while you're in the heat of serving orders. If you don't you'll definitely wish you had.

If you're new tell the guests. They won't think you're stupid! And don't feel stupid. We all had to start somewhere.

Don't cry, or get angry with a table because something went wrong. People have much more tolerance when they know they're dealing with a "rookie" and will remain calmer than they normal if things do go wrong. The dramatics really are unnecessary.

Make sure you always double back, and check yourself.

Your new, so just watch, and learn more than anything else. Ask lots of questions.

"Your a rookie, until you consider yourself otherwise."

CONCLUSION

We've finally come to the finish line! For this guide that is. Your skills as a waiter will grow as you grow. There's no limit to what you can learn from the principles within these pages. Have fun, and put your guests needs first.

ABOUT THE AUTHOR

Davon Thomas is currently living in New York city with his family. After leaving Delaware State University he has decided to pursue a career in filmmaking.